PRAYERS

for Eucharistic Adoration

Written and compiled by
Marie Paul Curley, FSP

Pauline
BOOKS & MEDIA
Boston

Nihil Obstat: Rev. Brian E. Mahoney, S.T.L.

Imprimatur: ✠ Most Rev. Seán O'Malley, O.F.M. Cap.
Archbishop of Boston
September 2, 2004

Cover photo: Mary Emmanuel Alves, FSP

ISBN 0-8198-5953-2

Copyright © 2004, Daughters of St. Paul

Published by Pauline Books & Media, 50 Saint Pauls Avenue, Boston, MA 02130-3491. Printed in U.S.A.

www.pauline.org

Pauline Books & Media is the publishing house of the Daughters of St. Paul, an international congregation of women religious serving the Church with the communications media.

7 8 9 10 11 12   20 19 18 17 16

Contents

෨෬

1

Invitation

∽∾∿

Then he took bread, blessed it, broke it, and gave it to them saying, "This is my body which is given up for you—do this in my remembrance." Likewise he took the cup after he had eaten and said, "This cup is the new covenant in my blood which is poured out for you."

—Luke 22:19–20*

∽∾∿

The Eucharist is one of the most tangible ways God is present in our world today. If confusion or loneliness weighs too heavily on our hearts, if we struggle with meaninglessness, if we long to step off life's frantic treadmill and slow down to ponder the direction of our lives—Jesus invites us, "Come to me."

At every Mass, or Eucharistic Celebration, we can discover anew how much our Triune God loves us. The Father sends his Beloved Son who shares our common humanity, walks with us, and shows us the way to the deepest possible fulfillment, and then gives himself completely to us, pouring out for love of us his very life in his passion, death, and resurrection, leaving with us the indwelling Spirit. It is Jesus' loving gift of his life, offering himself to the Father, that we participate in at every Eucharist: "This is my body and blood, given for you."

The Eucharist is God's greatest gift to us—it is where Jesus' heart meets the needs of the world on a daily basis. To faithfully live our Christian vocation, we need to be rooted in the Eucharist.

We center our lives in the Eucharist by giving priority to the Celebration of the Eucharist. The Sunday Eucharist becomes the center of our week; if we are able to attend daily Mass, it becomes the focal point of our day. Eucharistic adoration, or prayer before Jesus in the Blessed Sacrament, becomes a way to enrich our participation in the Eucharistic Celebration. Adoring Jesus in this way allows us personal time to more deeply immerse ourselves in the Paschal Mystery so that we begin to take on Jesus' own attitudes, way of life, and love for the Father.

From personal experience, I know how powerfully transforming Eucharistic adoration is. The deeper our Eucharistic prayer, the more fully we are able to participate in the Eucharistic Celebration and the more fully we are transformed in Christ—both in the liturgy we celebrate together and in our daily lives. Having discovered that in Christ we are God's beloved, we begin to fully live out our call to bring our world into deeper communion with Jesus, and, in him, with the Father and the Spirit.

May this booklet help you to begin or to enrich your Eucharistic prayer.

2

Prayer-Starters

෨෨

A morsel of bread is more real than the universe, more full of existence, more full of the Word—a song overflowing the sea, a mist confusing the sundial—God in exile.

— *Karol Wojtyla*

෨෨

For those times when we just have a few moments to pray, or when we feel distracted or too anxious to pray, "prayer-starters" entice us to enter into an encounter with Jesus.

෨

"Come to me, all you grown weary and
    burdened,
and I will refresh you.
Take my yoke upon you
and learn from me,
for I am gentle and humble hearted,
and you will find rest for your souls;
For my yoke is easy,
and my burden light."

— *Jesus (Mt 11:28–30*)*

෨

Pause before the tabernacle by yourself, for no special reason, even without saying a word, simply remaining in Christ's presence, contemplating the supreme gesture of love contained in the consecrated Bread.

— *Pope John Paul II*

———∾———

An Hour of Adoration prepares one for the celebration and reception of the Holy Eucharist. Frequent encounters and familiar conversation with Jesus produce friendship, resemblance, and identity of thought, feeling, and willing with Jesus.

— *Blessed James Alberione*

———∾———

I put before you the one great thing to love on earth: the Blessed Sacrament. There you will find romance, glory, honor, fidelity, and the true way of all your loves on earth and more than that.

— *J. R. R. Tolkien*

———∾———

Jesus is present and lives in our midst in the Eucharist. Let us listen to him for he is truth. Let us look at him, for he is the face of the Father. Let us love him, for he is love giving himself to his creatures. He comes to our soul so that it may disappear in him and become divine. What union, however great, can compare to this?

— *Saint Teresa de Los Andes*

———∾———

Jesus transforms a white particle into himself every day in order to communicate his life to you. What's more, with a love that is greater still, he wants to transform you into himself.

— *Saint Thérèse of Lisieux*

―――∽―――

"Abide in me as I abide in you. Just as the branch cannot bear fruit by itself unless it abides in the vine, neither can you unless you abide in me. I am the vine, you are the branches. Those who abide in me and I in them bear much fruit, because apart from me you can do nothing.... If you abide in me, and my words abide in you, ask for whatever you wish, and it will be done for you."

— *Jesus (Jn 15:4–7)*

―――∽―――

If we really love the good God, we will find it a joy and happiness to spend some time near him, to adore him, and keep company with so good a friend. He is there in the tabernacle. What is Jesus doing in this sacrament of love? He is loving us.

— *Saint John Vianney*

―――∽―――

Christ will not deceive us. That is why our lives must be woven around the Eucharist. The Christ who gives of himself to us under the appearance of bread and the Christ who is hidden under the distressing disguise of the poor is the same Jesus.

— *Blessed Teresa of Calcutta*

―――∽―――

To make room in our life for the Eucharistic Lord, so that he can change our life into his—is that asking too much?

— *Saint Edith Stein*

———∾———

"Could you not stay awake with me one hour?"

— *Jesus (Mt 26–40)*

———∾———

Be my life, my love, my all!

— *Saint Margaret Mary Alacoque*

———∾———

The LORD is my chosen portion and my cup.

— *Psalm 16:5*

———∾———

"I am the Way, the Truth, and the Life."

— *Jesus (Jn 14:6)*

———∾———

Realize that you may gain more in a quarter of an hour of prayer before the Blessed Sacrament than in all the other spiritual practices of the day.

— *Saint Alphonsus Liguori*

3

Eucharistic Readings

✎✎✎

Our present time and the future of the world
are illuminated by Christ's Eucharistic presence and are desperate for his action.

— *Blessed James Alberione*

✎✎✎

*These readings, intended to deepen our under-
standing of and appreciation for the Eucharistic
Mystery, can be used for meditation or to "set the
tone" for a longer time of prayer, such as an hour
of adoration.*

────✎────

I Am the Living Bread
Jesus (Jn 6:47–57)

"Very truly, I tell you, whoever believes has
eternal life. I am the bread of life. Your ancestors
ate the manna in the wilderness, and they died.
This is the bread that comes down from heaven,
so that one may eat of it and not die. I am the
living bread that came down from heaven. Whoever eats of this bread will live forever; and the
bread that I will give for the life of the world is
my flesh."

The Jews then disputed among themselves, saying, "How can this man give us his flesh to eat?" So Jesus said to them, "Very truly, I tell you, unless you eat the flesh of the Son of Man and drink his blood, you have no life in you. Those who eat my flesh and drink my blood have eternal life, and I will raise them up on the last day; for my flesh is true food and my blood is true drink. Those who eat my flesh and drink my blood abide in me, and I in them. Just as the living Father sent me, and I live because of the Father, so whoever eats me will live because of me."

Opening My Heart to Everyone
By Catherine de Hueck Doherty

Looking out of the window...I suddenly saw how tenderly, how gently, how warmly, how lovingly Christ bends toward the world. At that moment I also understood the words "cosmic charity," and when these words touched me, they expanded my heart to embrace especially all those who are weak and who keep on falling.

But then I looked again and I realized that everyone is weak and everyone falls! Does that mean that to be pure of heart one must love everyone? Yes...I have to open my heart to everyone who is weak, and that means *everyone*. Now I know why the pure of heart shall see God, and even see him now, *because he is in the ones who are weak.*

Yes, he will be in them, in each one of them, and that thought brought me to...the Eucharist. I saw the bread given to everyone present and I realized vividly and clearly that everyone among those present, including myself, was weak, prone to failing and falling again and again, and somehow I understood with the heart what the beatitude meant.

The Paschal Banquet
By Pope John Paul II

In instituting the Eucharist, Jesus did not merely say: "This is my body," "this is my blood," but went on to add: "which is given for you," "which is poured out for you" (Lk 22:19–20). Jesus did not simply state that what he was giving them to eat and drink was his Body and his Blood; he also expressed *its sacrificial meaning* and made sacramentally present his sacrifice which would soon be offered on the cross for the salvation of all.

The Church constantly draws her life from this redeeming sacrifice; she approaches it not only through faith-filled remembrance, but also through a real contact, since *this sacrifice is made present ever anew,* sacramentally perpetuated, in every community which offers it. The Eucharist thus applies to men and women today the reconciliation won once for all by Christ for mankind in every age.

The Lord wished to remain with us in the Eucharist, making his presence in meal and sacrifice the promise of a humanity renewed by his love.... Proclaiming the death of the Lord "until he comes" (1 Cor 11:26) entails that all who take part in the Eucharist be committed to changing their lives and making them in a certain way completely "Eucharistic."

———— ❧ ————

You Become the Body of Christ
By Saint Augustine of Hippo

By bread, you are instructed as to how you ought to cherish unity. Was that bread made of one grain of wheat? Were there not, rather, many grains? However, before they became bread, these grains were separate; they were joined together in water after a certain amount of crushing. For, unless the grain is ground and moistened with water, it cannot arrive at that form which is called bread.

So, too, you were previously ground, as it were, by the humiliation of your fasting and by the sacrament of exorcism. Then came the baptism of water; you were moistened, as it were, so to arrive at the form of bread. But without fire, bread does not exist. What, then, does fire signify? The chrism. For the sacrament of the Holy Spirit is the oil of our fire.... Therefore, the fire, that is, the Holy Spirit, comes after the water, then you become bread, that is, the body of Christ.

———— ❧ ————

An Extraordinary Incarnation
By Louise Perrotta

Every time we go to Mass, we hear the familiar words, "This is my body... This is my blood..." Do we ever find them odd? Do we ever ask what it means, really, to eat the Body and Blood of Christ?

Right from the early days of the Church, the very idea of eating Christ's Body made people uneasy. "I am the Bread of life," Jesus told a crowd. "My flesh is real food and my blood is true drink." People grew restless, disconcerted. "Does this shock you?" Jesus asked. It did.

In some ways, it would be more comforting to explain what goes on at Mass as mere symbolism. But the Catholic Church has always followed Jesus' lead, teaching that the consecrated bread and wine are transformed into Jesus' flesh and blood.

Exactly how the substance of bread and wine become the substance of Jesus' body is and always will be mystery. But then, so is the Incarnation. And isn't the mystery of the Eucharist in perfect continuity with the mystery of "God with us"? How consistent for a God who made a surprise appearance as a baby to continue his physical presence in an equally extraordinary way!

∽

Washing Each Others' Feet
By Ronald Rolheiser, OMI

We should be on our knees washing each others' feet because that is precisely what Jesus did at the first Eucharist, teaching us that the Eucharist is not a private act of devotion, meant to square our debts with God, but a call *to* and a grace *for* service. The Eucharist sends us out into the world ready to give expression to Christ's hospitality, humility, and self-effacement.

Where do we get such a notion? It lies at the very heart of the Eucharist itself. Jesus tells us this when he gives us the Eucharist, with the words: "Receive, give thanks, break, and share." The Eucharist invites us to receive nourishment from God, to be filled with gratitude, and, on the basis of that, to break open our lives and serve the poor in hospitality, humility, and self-donation.

It is no accident that, among all the potential scripture texts it might have picked for liturgy on Holy Thursday, the Church has chosen to use John's account of Jesus washing the feet of disciples. A splendid choice. Indeed, nothing better expresses the meaning of the Eucharist than does that gesture.

―――∾―――

Mary, Woman of the Eucharist
By Pope John Paul II

When, at the Visitation, Mary bore in her womb the Word made flesh, she became in some way a "tabernacle"—the first "tabernacle" in history—in which the Son of God, still invisible to our human gaze, allowed himself to be adored by Elizabeth, radiating his light as it were through the eyes and the voice of Mary. And is not the enraptured gaze of Mary as she contemplated the face of the newborn Christ and cradled him in her arms that unparalleled model of love which should inspire us every time we receive Eucharistic communion?

Mary, at the side of Christ throughout her life, made her own the sacrificial dimension of the Eucharist. The *Magnificat* expresses Mary's spirituality, and there is nothing greater than this spirituality for helping us to experience the mystery of the Eucharist. The Eucharist has been given to us so that our life, like that of Mary, may become completely a *Magnificat!*

I Am the Bread of Life
John 6:32–40

Jesus said to them, "Very truly, I tell you, it was not Moses who gave you the bread from heaven, but it is my Father who gives you the true bread from heaven. For the bread of God is that which comes down from heaven and gives life to the world."

They said to him, "Sir, give us this bread always." Jesus said to them, "I am the Bread of Life. Whoever comes to me will never be hungry, and whoever believes in me will never be thirsty. But I said to you that you have seen me and yet do not believe.

"Everything that the Father gives me will come to me, and anyone who comes to me I will never drive away...."

4

Eucharistic Prayers of Adoration

༄࿐

May I never leave you there alone but be
wholly present, my faith wholly vigilant,
wholly adoring, and wholly surrendered to
your creative action.

— *Blessed Elizabeth of the Trinity*

༄࿐

The Call

By George Herbert

Come, my Way, my Truth, my Life:
Such a Way, as gives us breath;
Such a Truth, as ends all strife;
And such a Life, as killeth death.

Come, my Light, my Feast, my Strength:
Such a Light, as shows a feast;
Such a Feast, as mends in length;
Such a Strength, as makes his guest.

Come, my Joy, my Love, my Heart:
Such a Joy, as none can move;
Such a Love, as none can part;
Such a Heart, as joys in love.

Prayer of Adoration
Adapted from Blessed James Alberione

Jesus, today's adoration is the meeting of my
    soul and all of my being with you.
I am the creature meeting the Creator;
the disciple before the Divine Master;
the patient with the Doctor of souls;
the poor one appealing to the Rich One;
the thirsty one drinking at the Font;
the weak before the Almighty;
the tempted seeking a sure Refuge;
the blind person searching for the Light;
the friend who goes to the True Friend;
the lost sheep sought by the Divine Shepherd;
the wayward heart who finds the Way;
the unenlightened one who finds Wisdom;
the bride who finds the Spouse of the soul;
the "nothing" who finds the All;
the afflicted who finds the Consoler;
the seeker who finds life's meaning.

Prayer for Faith in the Real Presence
Traditional

We come to you, dear Lord, like the apostles,
saying, "Increase our faith." Give us a strong
and lively faith that you are really present in the
Eucharist; an active faith that we may live by.

Give us the splendid faith of the centurion,
which drew such praise from you. Give us the
faith of the beloved disciple to recognize you and

say, "It is the Lord!" Give us the faith of Peter to confess, "You are Christ, the Son of the living God!" Give us the faith of Mary Magdalene to fall at your feet, crying, "Rabboni! Master!"

Give us the faith of all your saints to whom the Eucharist was heaven begun on earth. In every reception of the Eucharist and at every visit, increase our faith and love, our humility and reverence, and all good things will come to us.

Dearest Lord, increase our faith!

In Wonder
By Saint Teresa of Avila

O Wealth of the poor, how wonderfully can you sustain souls, revealing your great riches to them gradually and not permitting them to see them all at once! Since the time of that vision, I have never seen such great Majesty, hidden in a thing so small as the host, without marveling at your great wisdom.

My Soul Is Thirsting for You
Psalm 63:1–8

O God, you are my God, I seek you,
   my soul thirsts for you;
my flesh faints for you,
   as in a dry and weary land where there is no water.
So I have looked upon you in the sanctuary,
   beholding your power and glory.

Because your steadfast love is better than life,
  my lips will praise you.
So I will bless you as long as I live;
  I will lift up my hands and call on your name.

My soul is satisfied as with a rich feast,
  and my mouth praises you with joyful lips
when I think of you on my bed,
  and meditate on you in the watches of the
      night;
for you have been my help,
  and in the shadow of your wings I sing for joy.
My soul clings to you;
  your right hand upholds me.

_____❧_____

An Act of Love
by Saint John Vianney

I love you, O my God, and my only desire is to
love you until the last breath of my life. I love
you, O my infinitely lovable God, and I would
rather die loving you, than live without loving
you. I love you, Lord, and the only grace I ask is
to love you eternally.

My God, if my tongue cannot say in every moment that I love you, I want my heart to repeat it
to you as often as I draw breath.

5

Eucharistic Prayers of Praise and Thanksgiving

༄༅༅

O memorial of the wonders of God's love!

— *Saint Katharine Drexel*

༄༅༅

The Divine Praises
Traditional

Blessed be God.
Blessed be his Holy Name.
Blessed be Jesus Christ, true God and true Man.
Blessed be the name of Jesus.
Blessed be his most Sacred Heart.
Blessed be his most Precious Blood.
Blessed be Jesus in the most holy Sacrament of
   the Altar.
Blessed be the Holy Spirit the Paraclete.
Blessed be the great Mother of God, Mary most
   holy.
Blessed be her holy and Immaculate Conception.
Blessed be her glorious Assumption.
Blessed be the name of Mary, Virgin and Mother.
Blessed be Saint Joseph, her most chaste spouse.
Blessed be God in his angels and in his saints.

Fed by Your Bounty
By Jarena Lee

Lord, I have been fed with your bounty,
clothed with your mercy,
comforted by your love,
healed by your grace,
and upheld by your hand.

———— ❧ ————

Magnificat
Luke 1:46–55*

"My soul gives praise to the Lord,
  and my spirit rejoices in God my Savior;
Because he had regard for the lowliness of his
      handmaid,
  behold, henceforth all generations shall call
      me blessed,
for the Mighty One has done great things for me,
  and holy is his name,
and his mercy is from generation to generation
  toward those who fear him.
He has shown might with his arm,
  scattered the arrogant in the conceit of their
      heart,
he has pulled down the mighty from their thrones,
  and exalted the lowly,
the hungry he has filled with good things,
  and the rich he has sent away empty.
He has come to the aid of his servant, Israel,
  mindful of his mercy,
just as he promised our fathers,
  Abraham and his descendants forever."

———— ❧ ————

My Cup Overflows
Psalm 23

The LORD is my shepherd, I shall not want.
  He makes me lie down in green pastures;
he leads me beside still waters;
  he restores my soul.
He leads me in right paths
  for his name's sake.

Even though I walk through the darkest valley,
  I fear no evil;
for you are with me;
  your rod and your staff—
  they comfort me.

You prepare a table before me
  in the presence of my enemies;
you anoint my head with oil;
  my cup overflows.
Surely goodness and mercy shall follow me
  all the days of my life
and I shall dwell in the house of the LORD
  my whole life long.

Act of Trust in Jesus' Promises
By Marie Paul Curley, FSP

Jesus, I believe you are the Word who became
  flesh and lived among us, offering us grace
  and truth.
Jesus, I believe you are the Lamb of God who
  takes away our sins.

Jesus, I believe you are the Master who invites us to discipleship, growth, and an ever greater love.

Jesus, I believe you are God's beloved Son, sent into the world to save us.

Jesus, I believe you are Living Water, who quenches our thirst for meaning, love, peace, and truth, offering us abundant life!

Jesus, I believe you are the Bread of Life, broken and given for the life of the world.

Jesus, I believe you are the Light of the world, who frees us from darkness and answers the deepest questions of our hearts.

Jesus, I believe you are the Good Shepherd, who laid down his life for us and keeps us safe, and who calls us to shepherd others.

Jesus, I believe you are the Resurrection, promising eternal life to all who believe in you.

Jesus, I believe you are the Master who became the servant of all.

Jesus, I believe you are the living and true Vine who promises plentiful fruit and life.

Jesus, I believe you are the Way, the Truth, and the Life of the world, inviting us to be transformed in you.

The Richness of His Grace

Ephesians 1:3–23

Blessed be the God and Father of our Lord Jesus Christ, who has blessed us in Christ with every spiritual blessing in the heavenly places, just as he chose us in Christ before the foundation of the world to be holy and blameless before him in love. He destined us for adoption as his children through Jesus Christ, according to the good pleasure of his will, to the praise of his glorious grace that he freely bestowed on us in the Beloved. In him we have redemption through his blood, the forgiveness of our trespasses, according to the riches of his grace that he lavished on us.

With all wisdom and insight he has made known to us the mystery of his will, according to his good pleasure that he set forth in Christ, as a plan for the fullness of time, to gather up all things in him, things in heaven and things on earth. In Christ we have also obtained an inheritance, having been destined according to the purpose of him who accomplishes all things according to his counsel and will, so that we, who were the first to set our hope on Christ, might live for the praise of his glory.

6

Eucharistic Prayers for Conversion and Healing

ᢇᢍᢇ

God conquers evil with infinite mercy. It is in the face of this merciful love that a desire for conversion and a yearning for new life must be reawakened in us.

— *Pope John Paul II*

ᢇᢍᢇ

To Jesus, Good Shepherd
Adapted from Blessed James Alberione

Jesus, you are the Good Shepherd who gathers and cares for the scattered sheep. The shepherd leads and the sheep follow because they recognize the shepherd's voice. You have given your commandments, your counsels, your examples. Whoever heeds them is nourished with bread that does not perish: "My food is to do the will of the heavenly Father."

Have mercy on us when we try to nourish ourselves on falsehood or empty pleasures. Recall us to your way. Sustain us when we waver, strengthen us when we are weak. May everyone follow you, Shepherd and Guardian of our souls. You alone are the Way, you alone have words of

eternal life. We will follow you wherever you go.
Amen.

_____ ∽ _____

Act of Contrition
Traditional

My God,
I am sorry for my sins with all my heart.
In choosing to do wrong
and failing to do good,
I have sinned against you
whom I should love above all things.
I firmly intend, with your help,
to do penance,
to sin no more,
and to avoid whatever leads me to sin.
Our Savior Jesus Christ
suffered and died for us.
In his name, my God, have mercy.

_____ ∽ _____

Have Mercy
Psalm 51:1–2

Have mercy on me, O God,
    according to your steadfast love;
according to your abundant mercy
    blot out my transgressions.
Wash me thoroughly from my iniquity,
    and cleanse me from my sin.

_____ ∽ _____

To Return to You

By Francis Xavier Nguyen Van Thuan

Lord, grant me the strength to return to you,
like the prodigal son.
You are the principle of my life
and no one knows as well as you
what is most useful to me.
You have traced a path for each of us
in the plan of your love.
At each instant, we want to offer you our will.
In spite of ourselves,
we will not merely be resigned,
but as your children, we will be always available
  to your plan for us.
May your will be ours!

———∽———

Drawing Near to You

By Saint Thomas Aquinas

Almighty and eternal God, I approach the sacrament of your only-begotten Son, our Lord Jesus Christ. I am sick and draw near to the Physician of life; unclean to the Fountain of mercy; blind to the Light of eternal brightness; poor and needy to the Lord of heaven and earth.

I ask you, in your abundant goodness, to heal my sickness, cleanse my sinfulness, enlighten my blindness, enrich my poverty, and clothe my nakedness.

Make me ready to receive the Bread of angels, the King of kings and Lord of lords, with reverence and humility, contrition and love, purity and faith, with the purpose and intention necessary for the good of my soul.... Grant that I may be worthy to be incorporated into his Mystical Body and counted among his members.

_____∾_____

Heal Me, O Lord
Adapted from Jeremiah 17:14

Heal me, O Lord.
Save me and give me peace!

_____∾_____

To Jesus Crucified
Traditional

Behold, my beloved and good Jesus,
I kneel before you,
asking you most earnestly
to engrave upon my heart
a deep and lively faith, hope, and charity,
with true repentance for my sins,
and a firm resolve to make amends.
As I reflect upon your five wounds,
and dwell upon them with deep compassion
    and grief,
I recall, good Jesus, the words the prophet
    David spoke long ago:
They have pierced my hands and my feet,
they have counted all my bones!

7

Eucharistic Prayers of Intercession

ᴄᴡᴄᴡ

Be "big-hearted" enough in prayer to embrace everyone in the world.

— *Venerable Mother Thecla Merlo*

ᴄᴡᴄᴡ

The intercessory prayers included here are for personal transformation, for loved ones and special needs, and for the coming of the kingdom of God.

I Believe in Your Steadfast Love
Prayer For Special Needs
By Mary Elizabeth Tebo, FSP

Jesus, present in a special way in the Eucharist, I come to talk with you about a special need. Like Solomon who asked for wisdom, and received everything else besides, I, too, ask for your abundant blessings. Lord, I desire wisdom and compassion, and, in particular, I confide to you my special need: (here, mention your need). I trust in your assurance that not even a sparrow falls to the ground without your Father's knowledge. Therefore, I wait upon your mercy, for I believe that you will answer me. Amen.

Anima Christi
Traditional

Soul of Christ, sanctify me.
Body of Christ, save me.
Blood of Christ, inebriate me.
Water flowing from the side of Christ, wash me.
Passion of Christ, strengthen me.
Good Jesus, hear me.
Within your wounds, hide me
and keep me close to thee.
From the evil enemy defend me.
In the hour of my death, call me
and bid me come to thee,
that with thy saints I may praise thee
through all eternity.

Make Me an Instrument of Your Peace
By Saint Francis of Assisi

Lord, make me an instrument of your peace:
where there is hatred, let me sow love;
where there is discord, unity;
where there is injury, pardon;
where there is error, truth;
where there is doubt, faith;
where there is despair, hope;
where there is darkness, light;
where there is sadness, joy.

Divine Master,
grant that I may not so much seek
to be consoled as to console;

to be understood, as to understand;
to be loved, as to love.
For it is in giving that we receive;
it is in forgetting self that we find ourselves;
it is in pardoning that we are pardoned;
and it is in dying that we are born to eternal
    life.

———∾———

Invocations to Jesus Master
By Blessed James Alberione

Jesus Master, sanctify my mind and increase my faith. Jesus teaching in the Church, draw everyone to yourself. Jesus Master, deliver me from error, empty thoughts, and eternal blindness.

Jesus, Way between the Father and us, I offer you everything and await all from you. Jesus, Way of sanctity, help me imitate you faithfully. Jesus Way, may I respond wholeheartedly to the Father's call to holiness.

Jesus Life, live in me so that I may live in you.

Jesus Life, do not ever permit anything to separate me from you. Jesus Life, grant that I may live eternally in the joy of your love.

Jesus Truth, may you shine in the world through me. Jesus Way, may I be a faithful mirror of your example for others. Jesus Life, may I be a channel of your grace and consolation to others.

———∾———

To Foster Respect for Life
By Pope John Paul II

O Mary, bright dawn of the new world, Mother of the living, to you do we entrust the cause of life: Look down, O Mother, upon the vast numbers of babies not allowed to be born, of the poor whose lives are made difficult, of men and women who are victims of brutal violence, of the elderly and the sick killed by indifference or out of misguided mercy. Grant that all who believe in your Son may proclaim the Gospel of life with honesty and love to the people of our time. Obtain for them the grace to accept that Gospel as a gift ever new, the joy of celebrating it with gratitude throughout their lives, and the courage to bear witness to it resolutely, in order to build, together with all people of good will, the civilization of truth and love, to the praise and glory of God, the Creator and lover of life.

For Friends and Loved Ones
By Saint Gertrude the Great and Saint Mechtilde

Lord, I see clearly that any affection which I have ever had is scarcely as one drop in the vast ocean of all the seas, when compared with the tenderness of thy divine heart toward those whom I love.... Therefore I cannot even by one thought wish anything other than that which thy almighty wisdom has appointed for each of them.... Lord, bless thy special friends and mine, according to the good pleasure of thy divine goodness.

For the Needs of Others
By Saint Anselm

God of love, whose compassion never fails,
we bring you the sufferings of the world;
the needs of the homeless,
the cries of prisoners,
the pains of the sick and injured,
the sorrow of the bereaved,
the helplessness of the elderly and weak.
According to their needs and your great mercy,
strengthen and relieve them
in Jesus Christ our Lord.

Is My Life Too "Safe," O Lord?
By Francis Xavier Nguyen Van Thuan

Grant, Lord, that we may offer the Eucharistic sacrifice with great love. If we do not offer ourselves with Jesus in some way: if our lives are safe from hunger, thirst, cold, and humiliation; if our faces are not struck by slaps and spittle; if a crown of thorns is not inflicted upon us; if we do not carry the cross, are not nailed to it, do not die on it; and if we are not buried in another's tomb, then we must be transformed. If because of fear I try to escape Jesus' destiny, then despite all the rites I follow and their solemnity, I am not offering the Eucharistic sacrifice with Jesus' sentiments.

Embrace the Whole World
By Saint Faustina Kowalska

O living Host, my one and only Strength, Fountain of love and mercy, embrace the whole world, fortify those who are weak! (Diary, no. 223)

———∽———

Prayer for Unity
By Basil Hume

Lord Jesus Christ, you said may they all be one, just as, Father, you are in me and I am in you, so that the world may believe it was you who sent me.

Dear Lord, bring together in love and peace all who believe in you. Amen.

8

A Guide to Making an Hour of Adoration

༺࿐༻

Blessed James Alberione (1884–1971), priest and founder of the Pauline Family, daily celebrated the Eucharist and spent four to five hours in adoration. The Eucharist was central to his day, sustaining an active apostolic lifestyle. Blessed James developed a Pauline method of Eucharistic adoration that is scripturally based and easy to use.

At the center of Blessed James Alberione's Eucharistic spirituality is Jesus, our Way, Truth, and Life. Jesus not only proclaims the truth, but is himself our *Truth* because in him we discover the loving face of God. Jesus is the *Way* to the Father by his example, but also because he walks with us on our journey. As our *Life*, Jesus saves us from sin and invites us to experience the fullness of life in him. Our deepening relationship with Jesus, Way, Truth, and Life, transforms us and our relationships: we become more loving and committed to advancing peace and justice in our world.

The Pauline hour of adoration is divided into three parts or "moments," based on Jesus' definition of himself as Way, Truth, and Life.

———•———

First Moment

Adoring Jesus Truth

We listen attentively to God's Word to us to-day and let his truth shape our minds and attitudes.

As we begin the hour of adoration, we choose a theme or recall a particular need to bring to prayer.

- Begin with a hymn or prayer of adoration;
- Ask for the light of the Holy Spirit;
- Choose and read a passage of Scripture (or another reading from Chapter 3);
- Listen with your heart to how Jesus is speaking to you in his Word;
- Converse with Jesus about how this reading touches your life;
- Make a personal act of faith.

———⌇———

Second Moment

Following Jesus Way

In light of our reading, we turn to contemplate Jesus our Way and Model, looking more closely at our relationship with him.

- Contemplate God's action in your life, thanking God for the marvelous ways he has gifted you.
- Again, ask for the light from the Holy Spirit, who searches our hearts.

- Confront your life with Jesus' words and example, express sorrow for your sinfulness, and resolve to follow Jesus faithfully.
- Renew your trust in God's great love for you.

———∾———

Third Moment

Sharing Jesus' Life

Converted anew, we open our hearts to Jesus Life, to let his sustaining grace and peace fill us so that we can bring that same peace and love to others.

- Rejoice in Jesus' presence and love for you, inviting him to transform you.
- Invite Jesus into your heart and share your deepest desires.
- Bring to God your needs and those of the world.
- Pray spontaneously or use a psalm, the Liturgy of the Hours, the Rosary, the Stations of the Cross, or another favorite prayer.
- Conclude with an act of love and offer Jesus one way you can be his presence in the world.

(Note: If you find this outline helpful, you may find a fuller explanation of the Pauline hour of adoration in the book Life for the World, *which includes twelve hours of adoration for personal or group use.)*

———∾———

9

An Hour of Adoration

༺~~༻

Jesus, Our Way, Truth, and Life

Theme: To be transformed in Christ

During the Last Supper, Jesus spoke from his heart to his disciples. Take a few moments to adore Jesus who died and rose for you, who wants so much to be part of your life that he nourishes you in Communion, who wants so much to be close to you that he remains present here in the Eucharist in silence and simplicity.

༺~~༻

Adoring Jesus Truth

Ask the Holy Spirit, whom Jesus gave to us as our "Intercessor" before the Father, to flood your soul with divine light.

Reading
John 14:1–7*

"Let not your hearts be troubled!
Believe in God and believe in me.
In my Father's house are many rooms;
were it not so, would I have told you that I'm
    going to prepare a place for you?

And if I go and prepare a place for you,
I will come again and take you to myself,
so that where I am, you, too, may be.
Yet where I am going, you know the way."

Thomas said to him, "Lord, we don't know where
    you're going! How can we know the way?"
Jesus said to him,
"I am the way and the truth and the life;
no one comes to the Father except through me.
If you know me, you will know the Father, too,
and from now on you will know him and will
    see him."

Reflection

In this powerful yet consoling passage, Jesus
invites you to enter more deeply into a personal
relationship with him—a relationship that can
encompass any pressure, any difficulty, any joy or
trouble. Jesus wants you to experience the secu-
rity of being loved faithfully, unconditionally:
"Let not your hearts be troubled!"

The words, "I am the Way, the Truth, and the
Life," are not only a profound self-definition and
a description of Jesus' relationship with us, they
are also a dazzling yet mysterious promise of loving fidelity and companionship. What might these
words of Jesus mean to you? How is Jesus your
Way, your Truth, and your Life? How can you enter more deeply into relationship with Jesus?

*As a response to the reading, renew your faith in
Jesus with the prayer "Act of Trust in Jesus'
Promises," on page 20.*

———∽———

Following Jesus Way

To "remain" in Jesus means to let our entire life be shaped by the absolutely faithful love of a God who pours himself out for the beloved.

Reflect on the ways God has poured out blessings on you: in your family, in your friendships, in your life of faith, in your vocation. How has God worked in you and through you? In your accomplishments, in your weaknesses? In the past day, week, or month?

In gratitude, pray the poem, "The Call," on page 14.

Pondering the mystery of Jesus' Eucharistic love for us, we realize that we, too, are called to pour ourselves out in love for God and for those whom God loves. Jesus said, "Whoever keeps my commandments and obeys them—he it is who loves me, while whoever loves me is loved by my Father, and I will love him and reveal myself to him" (Jn 14:21*).

Pause to reflect: How is the Lord inviting you to love more deeply, as he loves you?

For the times you have not loved as the Lord would have, pray this act of sorrow:

Lord, you have called me "friend" and "beloved," even though you know I am weak and sinful. I am deeply sorry for my sins, for having broken or weakened my communion with you and with your beloved ones—each person made in your image. I pray that your loving mercy will heal what I have hurt, strengthen what I have weakened, and transform me into a more faithful reflection of your love upon earth.

Ask Jesus, the Divine Master, to pour out his grace upon you in a very special way today, to bring you to the deepest core of your vocation of living in him.

———∾———

Sharing Jesus' Life

Prayer nurtures our growth in holiness. This chaplet was developed by Blessed James Alberione to nurture Christ's life in us. Use one or each point of the chaplet as a "launching pad" to pray in your own words your desire for Christ to live in you—mind, will, and heart.

Chaplet to Jesus, Way, Truth, and Life

Adapted from Blessed James Alberione

1. We Adore You, Jesus Truth

Jesus, Divine Master, we adore you as the Word Incarnate sent by the Father to teach us life-giving truths. You alone have words of eternal life. We believe in you and the teachings of the Church, and we pray that your Word may enlighten our minds. Master, show us the treasures of your wisdom; let us know the Father; make us your true disciples. Increase our faith so that we may reach eternal life in heaven.

2. We Adore You, Jesus Way

Jesus, Divine Master, we adore you as the Beloved of the Father, the sole Way to him. We contemplate you throughout your earthly life. We want to follow your teachings and example, treating everyone with love and respect. Draw us to yourself, so that by following in your footsteps, we may seek only your will. Increase hope in us and the desire to be similar to you, so that we may rejoice to hear your words: "Just as you did it to one of the least of these...you did it to me" (Mt 25:34, 40).

3. Live in Us, Jesus

Jesus, Divine Master, we adore you as the only-begotten Son of God, who came on earth to give abundant life to humanity. We thank you because by your death on the cross, you give us life through Baptism and you nourish us in the Eucharist and in the other sacraments. Live in us, O Jesus, with the outpouring of the Holy Spirit, so that we may love you with our whole mind, strength, and heart, and love our neighbor as ourselves for love of you. Increase charity in us, so that one day we may all be united with you in the eternal happiness of heaven.

4. We Adore You Living in the Church

Jesus, Divine Master, we adore you living in the Church, the Mystical Body of Christ, through which you bring us to eternal life. We thank you for having joined us together as members of the Church, in which you continue to be for humanity the Way, the Truth, and the Life. We ask that those who do not believe may receive the gift of faith, that those who are separated may be brought into full communion, and that all people be united in faith, in a common hope, in charity. Assist the Church and its leaders; sustain the People of God. Lord Jesus, our wish is yours: that there be one fold under one Shepherd, so that we may all be together in heaven.

5. *Jesus, May We Radiate You*

Jesus, Divine Master, we adore you with the angels who sang the reasons for your Incarnation: glory to God and peace to all people. We thank you for having called us to share in your saving mission. Enkindle in us your flame of love for God and for all humanity. Live in us so that we may radiate you through our prayer, suffering, and work, as well as by word, example, and deed. Send good laborers into your harvest. Come, Master and Lord! Teach and reign through Mary, Mother, Teacher, and Queen.

As you conclude, ask Jesus to allow you to reflect his love to everyone you meet today, especially to the first person you come across who seems "unlovable."

10

Eucharistic Hymns

～∾∾

Humbly Let Us Voice Our Homage
Tantum Ergo Sacramentum
By Saint Thomas Aquinas

Humbly let us voice our homage
for so great a Sacrament:
let all former rites surrender
to the Lord's New Testament;
what our senses fail to fathom
let us grasp through faith's consent.

Glory, honor, adoration,
let us sing with one accord.
Praised be God almighty Father;
praised be Christ, his Son, our Lord;
praised be God the Holy Spirit;
Triune Godhead be adored. Amen.

Tantum ergo Sascraméntum
venerémur cérnui;
et antíquum documéntum,
novo cedat rítui;
praestet fides suppleméntum,
sénsuum deféctui.

Genitóri, genitóque,
laus et jubilátio,

salus, honor, virtus quoque
sit et benedíctio:
procedénti ab utróque
compar sit laudátio. Amen.

———∾———

O Saving Victim, Opening Wide
(O Salutaris Hostia)
Traditional

O Saving Victim, opening wide
The gate of heav'n to man below!
Our foes press on from ev'ry side:
Thine aid supply, Thy strength bestow.

To Thy great name be endless praise,
Immortal Godhead, one in three;
Oh, grant us endless length of days
In our true native land with Thee. Amen.

O Salutáris Hóstia
Quae caeli pandis óstium.
Bella premunt hostília,
Da robur, fer auxílium.

Uni trinóque Domino
Sit sempitérna glória.
Qui vitam sine término
Nobis donet in pátria. Amen.

BOOKS & MEDIA

The Daughters of St. Paul operate book and media centers at the following addresses. Visit, call or write the one nearest you today, or find us at www.paulinestore.org.

CALIFORNIA
3908 Sepulveda Blvd, Culver City, CA 90230   310-397-8676
3250 Middlefield Road, Menlo Park, CA 94025   650-369-4230

FLORIDA
145 S.W. 107th Avenue, Miami, FL 33174   305-559-6715

HAWAII
1143 Bishop Street, Honolulu, HI 96813   808-521-2731

ILLINOIS
172 North Michigan Avenue, Chicago, IL 60601   312-346-4228

LOUISIANA
4403 Veterans Memorial Blvd, Metairie, LA 70006 504-887-7631

MASSACHUSETTS
885 Providence Hwy, Dedham, MA 02026   781-326-5385

MISSOURI
9804 Watson Road, St. Louis, MO 63126   314-965-3512

NEW YORK
64 W. 38th Street, New York, NY 10018   212-754-1110

SOUTH CAROLINA
243 King Street, Charleston, SC 29401   843-577-0175

TEXAS
Currently no book center; for parish exhibits or outreach evangelization, contact: 210-569-0500, or SanAntonio@paulinemedia.com, or P.O. Box 761416, San Antonio, TX 78245

VIRGINIA
1025 King Street, Alexandria, VA 22314   703-549-3806

CANADA
3022 Dufferin Street, Toronto, ON M6B 3T5   416-781-9131